All Ladybird books are available at most bookshops, supermarkets and newsagents, or can be ordered direct from:

Ladybird Postal Sales
PO Box 133 Paignton TQ3 2YP England
Telephone: (+44) 01803 554761 • *Fax:* (+44) 01803 663394

A catalogue record for this book is available from the British Library

Published by Ladybird Books Ltd • A subsidiary of the Penguin Group • A Pearson Company
© LADYBIRD BOOKS LTD MCMXCIX

100
Favourite
Nursery
Rhymes

illustrated by Marjolein Pottie

Ladybird

Rhymes in this book:

Mary had a little lamb,
Its fleece was white as snow,
And everywhere that Mary went
The lamb was sure to go.

Little Bo-Peep has lost her sheep,
And doesn't know where to find them.
Leave them alone, and they'll come home,
Bringing their tails behind them.

Little Miss Muffet
Sat on a tuffet,
Eating her curds and whey.
There came a big spider,
Who sat down beside her,
And frightened Miss Muffet away.

Lucy Locket lost her pocket,
Kitty Fisher found it.
Not a penny was there in it,
Only ribbon round it.

Curly Locks, Curly Locks, will you be mine?
You shall not wash dishes, nor yet feed the swine,
But sit on a cushion and sew a fine seam,
And feast upon strawberries, sugar and cream.

Mary, Mary, quite contrary,
How does your garden grow?
With silver bells and cockle shells,
And pretty maids all in a row!

Little Poll Parrot
Sat in her garret
Eating toast and tea.
A little brown mouse
Jumped into the house
And stole it all away.

Bye, Baby Bunting,
Daddy's gone a-hunting,
Gone to get a rabbit skin
To wrap the Baby Bunting in.

Three little ghosties,
Sat on three posties,
Eating buttered toasties,
Greasing their fisties
Up to their wristies.
Weren't they beasties
To make such feasties!

Little Tommy Tucker
Sings for his supper.
What shall he eat?
White bread and butter.

How will he cut it
Without a knife?
How will he marry
Without a wife?

Little Boy Blue, come blow your horn!
The sheep's in the meadow,
The cow's in the corn.
Where is the boy who looks after the sheep?
He's under the haycock, fast asleep.
Will you wake him? No, not I!
For if I do, he's sure to cry.

Simple Simon met a pieman,
Going to the fair.
Says Simple Simon to the pieman,
'Let me taste your ware.'

Says the pieman to Simple Simon,
'Show me first your penny.'
Says Simple Simon to the pieman,
'Indeed I have not any.'

Little Jack Horner sat in a corner,
Eating his Christmas pie.
He put in his thumb,
And pulled out a plum,
And said, 'What a good boy am I!'

Tom, Tom, the piper's son,
Stole a pig and away did run.
The pig was eat,
And Tom was beat,
And Tom went howling down the street.

Dance to your daddy,
My little laddie,
Dance to your daddy,
My little lamb.

You shall have a fishy
In a little dishy,
You shall have a fishy
When the boat comes in.

Georgie Porgie, pudding and pie,
Kissed the girls and made them cry.
When the boys came out to play,
Georgie Porgie ran away.

See-saw, Margery Daw,
Johnny shall have a new master.
He shall have but a penny a day,
Because he can't work any faster.

Jack be nimble,
Jack be quick,
Jack jump over
The candlestick.

Jack and Jill went up the hill
To fetch a pail of water.
Jack fell down and broke his crown,
And Jill came tumbling after.

I had a little nut tree,
Nothing would it bear
But a silver nutmeg
And a golden pear.

The King of Spain's daughter
Came to visit me,
And all for the sake
Of my little nut tree.

Lavender's blue, dilly-dilly,
Rosemary's green,
When I am King, dilly-dilly,
You shall be Queen.

Baa, baa, black sheep, have you any wool?
Yes, sir, yes, sir, three bags full.
One for the master, and one for the dame,
And one for the little boy who lives in the lane.

Goosey, goosey, gander,
Where shall I wander?
Upstairs, downstairs,
In my lady's chamber.
There I met an old man
Who would not say his prayers.
I took him by the left leg
And threw him down the stairs.

Hey, diddle, diddle,
The cat and the fiddle,
The cow jumped over the moon.
The little dog laughed
To see such fun,
And the dish ran away with the spoon!

Ride a cockhorse to Banbury Cross,
To see a fine lady upon a white horse.
Rings on her fingers and bells on her toes,
And she shall have music wherever she goes.

Doctor Foster went to Gloucester
In a shower of rain.
He stepped in a puddle, right up to his middle,
And never went there again.

Humpty Dumpty sat on a wall,
Humpty Dumpty had a great fall.
All the King's horses
And all the King's men
Couldn't put Humpty
    together again.

Rub-a-dub-dub,
Three men in a tub,
And who do you think they be?
The butcher, the baker,
The candlestick-maker,
Turn them out, knaves all three.

Bobby Shaftoe's gone to sea,
Silver buckles on his knee.
He'll come back and marry me,
Bonny Bobby Shaftoe!

Old Mother Hubbard
Went to the cupboard
To fetch her poor dog a bone.
But when she got there
The cupboard was bare,
And so the poor dog had none.

There was a crooked man,
And he walked a crooked mile.
He found a crooked sixpence
Against a crooked stile.
He bought a crooked cat,
Which caught a crooked mouse,
And they all lived together
In a little crooked house.

There was an old woman tossed up in a blanket,
Seventeen times as high as the moon.
But where she was going no one could tell,
For under her arm she carried a broom.
'Old woman, old woman, old woman,' said I,
'Where are you going to up so high?'
'To sweep the cobwebs from the sky,
And I'll be with you by and by!'

The Queen of Hearts
She made some tarts,
All on a summer's day.
The Knave of Hearts
He stole the tarts,
And took them clean away.

Hickory, dickory, dock,
The mouse ran up the clock.
The clock struck one,
The mouse ran down.
Hickory, dickory, dock!

Cobbler, cobbler, mend my shoe,
Get it done by half past two.
Stitch it up and stitch it down
And then I'll give you half a crown.

Six little mice sat down to spin.
Pussy passed by and she peeped in,
'What are you doing, my little men?'
'Weaving coats for gentlemen.'
'Shall I come in and cut off your threads?'
'No, no, Mistress Pussy, you'll bite off our heads!'
'Oh no, I'll not, I'll help you to spin.'
'That may be so, but don't you come in.'

I love little pussy, her coat is so warm,
And if I don't hurt her, she'll do me no harm.
So I'll not pull her tail, nor drive her away,
But pussy and I very gently will play.

Three blind mice,
Three blind mice,
See how they run!
See how they run!
They all ran after the farmer's wife,
Who cut off their tails with a carving knife.
Did ever you see such a thing in your life,
As three blind mice?

Cock-a-doodle-doo!
My dame has lost her shoe,
My master's lost his fiddling stick
And doesn't know what to do.

Ladybird, ladybird, fly away home,
Your house is on fire and your children all gone.
All but one, and her name is Ann,
And she crept under the frying pan.

Ding, dong, bell,
Pussy's in the well.
Who put her in?
Little Johnny Green.
Who pulled her out?
Little Tommy Stout.
What a naughty boy was that
To try to drown poor pussy cat,
Who never did him any harm,
But killed the mice in father's barn.

A cat came fiddling out of a barn,
With a pair of bagpipes under her arm.
She could sing nothing but fiddle-cum-fee,
The mouse has married the bumblebee.
Pipe, cat! Dance, mouse!
We'll have a wedding at our good house.

Pussycat, pussycat, where have you been?
'I've been to London to visit the Queen.'
Pussycat, pussycat, what did you there?
'I frightened a little mouse under the chair.'

Hickety, pickety, my black hen,
She lays eggs for gentlemen.
Sometimes nine, and sometimes ten,
Hickety, pickety, my black hen.

There was an old woman who lived in a shoe,
She had so many children she didn't know what to do.
She gave them some broth without any bread,
Then scolded them soundly and sent them to bed.

Jack Sprat could eat no fat,
His wife could eat no lean,
And so between them both,
They licked the platter clean.

Pease porridge hot,
Pease porridge cold,
Pease porridge in the pot,
Nine days old.

Some like it hot,
Some like it cold,
Some like it in the pot,
Nine days old.

The lion and the unicorn were fighting for the crown,
The lion beat the unicorn all round the town.
Some gave them white bread and some gave them brown,
And some gave them plum cake and drummed them out of town.

Oh, have you seen the muffin man,
The muffin man, the muffin man?
Oh, have you seen the muffin man
Who lives in Drury Lane?

One, two,
Buckle my shoe;

Three, four,
Knock at the door;

Five, six,
Pick up sticks;

Seven, eight,
Lay them straight;

Nine, ten,
A big fat hen.

Gregory Griggs, Gregory Griggs,
Had twenty-seven different wigs;
He wore them up, he wore them down,
To please the people of the town;
He wore them east, he wore them west,
But he never could tell which he loved the best.

This old man, he played one,
He played nick-nack
On my drum!
Nick-nack-paddy-whack
Give a dog a bone,
This old man came rolling home.

Rain on the green grass,
And rain on the tree,
Rain on the house-top,
But not on me.

It's raining, it's pouring,
The old man is snoring;
He went to bed
And bumped his head,
And couldn't get up in the morning.

Peter Piper picked a peck of pickled pepper;
A peck of pickled pepper Peter Piper picked.
If Peter Piper picked a peck of pickled pepper,
Where's the peck of pickled pepper Peter Piper picked?

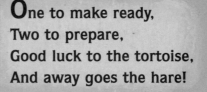

One to make ready,
Two to prepare,
Good luck to the tortoise,
And away goes the hare!

Roses are red,
Violets are blue,
Sugar is sweet
And so are you.

Betty Botter bought some butter,
'But,' she said, 'the butter's bitter;
If I put it in my batter
It will make my batter bitter,
But a bit of better butter,
That would make my batter better.'
So she bought a bit of butter
Better than her bitter butter,
And she put it in her batter,
And the batter was not bitter.
So it was better Betty Botter
Bought a bit of better butter.

Two legs sat upon three legs
With one leg in his lap.
In comes four legs
And runs away with one leg.
Up jumps two legs,
Picks up three legs,
Throws it after four legs,
And makes him bring one leg back.

If all the world were paper,
And all the sea were ink,
And all the trees were bread and cheese,
What should we have to drink?

She sells seashells on the seashore;
The shells she sells are seashells I'm sure.
So if she sells seashells on the seashore,
I'm sure the shells are seashore shells.

Monday's child is fair of face,
Tuesday's child is full of grace,
Wednesday's child is full of woe,
Thursday's child has far to go,
Friday's child is loving and giving,
Saturday's child works hard for its living,
But the child that's born on the Sabbath day
Is bonny and bright, and good and gay.

One for sorrow, two for joy,
Three for a girl, four for a boy,
Five for silver, six for gold,
Seven for a secret never to be told.

Thirty days has September,
April, June and November,
All the rest have thirty-one,
Excepting February alone,
And that has twenty-eight days clear,
And twenty-nine in each leap year.

Solomon Grundy,
Born on Monday,
Christened on Tuesday,
Married on Wednesday,
Took ill on Thursday,
Worse on Friday,
Died on Saturday,
Buried on Sunday,
That was the end
Of Solomon Grundy.

Five little peas in a peapod pressed;
One grew, two grew and so did all the rest.
They grew and grew and did not stop,
Until one day the peapod popped.

The wheels on the bus
Go round and round,
Round and round,
Round and round.
The wheels on the bus
Go round and round,
All day long.

The horn on the bus
Goes peep, peep, peep... etc.

The people on the bus
Bounce up and down... etc.

Miss Polly had a dolly
Who was sick, sick, sick.
So she called for the doctor
To be quick, quick, quick.

The doctor came
With his bag and his hat,
And he knocked on the door
With a rat-tat-tat.

He looked at the dolly
And he shook his head.
Then he said, 'Miss Polly,
Put her straight to bed.'

He wrote on a paper
For a pill, pill, pill,
'I'll be back in the morning
With my bill, bill, bill.'

Down at the station, early in the morning,
See the little puffer-trains all in a row;
See the engine-driver pull his little lever –
Puff puff, peep peep, off we go!

Heads, shoulders, knees and toes,
Knees and toes.
Heads, shoulders, knees and toes,
Knees and toes,
And eyes and ears and mouth and nose,
Heads, shoulders, knees and toes.

Pat-a-cake, pat-a-cake, baker's man!
Bake me a cake as fast as you can.
Roll it and pat it and mark it with B,
And put it in the oven for baby and me.

Five little ducks went swimming one day,
Over the hills and far away.
Mother Duck said, 'Quack, quack, quack, quack,'
And only four little ducks came back.

Four little ducks went swimming one day... etc.

Three little ducks went swimming one day... etc.

Two little ducks went swimming one day... etc.

One little duck went swimming one day... etc.

And five little ducks came swimming back.

One potato, two potato,
Three potato, four,
Five potato, six potato,
Seven potato, more.

Polly put the kettle on,
Polly put the kettle on,
Polly put the kettle on,
We'll all have tea.

Sukey take it off again,
Sukey take it off again,
Sukey take it off again,
They've all gone away.

I'm a little teapot,
Short and stout.
Here's my handle,
Here's my spout.
When I see the teacups
Hear me shout,
'Tip me up and pour me out!'

One, two, three, four, five,
Once I caught a fish alive,
Six, seven, eight, nine, ten.
Then I let it go again.
Why did you let it go?
Because it bit my finger so.
Which finger did it bite?
This little finger on the right.

Row, row, row your boat,
Gently down the stream.
Merrily, merrily, merrily, merrily,
Life is but a dream.

This is the way the ladies ride,
Nimble, nimble, nimble, nimble.
This is the way the gentlemen ride,
A gallop, a trot, a gallop, a trot.
This is the way the farmers ride,
Jiggety-jog, jiggety-jog.
And when they come to a hedge – they jump over!
And when they come to a slippery spot
They scramble, scramble, scramble,
Tumble-down bump!

Horsie, horsie, don't you stop,
Just let your feet go clippety-clop.
Your tail goes swish, and the wheels go round –
Giddy up, we're homeward bound!

Incy Wincy Spider
Climbing up the spout.
Down came the rain
And washed the spider out.
Out came the sunshine
And dried up all the rain,
So Incy Wincy Spider
Climbed up the spout again.

Two little dickey birds sitting on a wall,
One named Peter, one named Paul.
Fly away, Peter! Fly away, Paul!
Come back, Peter! Come back, Paul!

Oh, the grand old Duke of York,
He had ten thousand men.
He marched them up to the top of the hill,
And he marched them down again.
And when they were up, they were up,
And when they were down, they were down,
And when they were only halfway up,
They were neither up nor down!

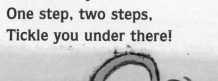

Teddy bear, teddy bear,
Turn around.
Teddy bear, teddy bear,
Touch the ground.

Teddy bear, teddy bear,
Climb the stairs.
Teddy bear, teddy bear,
Say your prayers.

Teddy bear, teddy bear,
Turn out the light.
Teddy bear, teddy bear,
Say good night.

Round and round the garden,
Like a teddy bear.
One step, two steps,
Tickle you under there!

To market, to market, to buy a fat pig,
Home again, home again, jiggety-jig.
To market, to market, to buy a fat hog,
Home again, home again, jiggety-jog.

This little pig went to market,
This little pig stayed at home.
This little pig had roast beef,
This little pig had none.
And this little pig cried, 'Wee-wee-wee,'
All the way home.

Here we go round the mulberry bush,
The mulberry bush, the mulberry bush.
Here we go round the mulberry bush,
On a cold and frosty morning.

Ring a ring o' roses,
A pocket full of posies.
A-tishoo! A-tishoo!
We all fall down.

'Oranges and lemons,'
Say the bells of St Clement's.

'You owe me five farthings,'
Say the bells of St Martin's.

'When will you pay me?'
Say the bells of Old Bailey.

'When I grow rich,'
Say the bells at Shoreditch.

'Pray, when will that be?'
Say the bells of Stepney.

'I'm sure I don't know,'
Says the great bell at Bow.

Here comes a candle
To light you to bed.
Here comes a chopper
To chop off your head.

London Bridge is falling down,
Falling down, falling down,
London Bridge is falling down,
My fair lady.

The big ship sails on the alley-alley-o, the alley-alley-o, the alley-alley-o,
The big ship sails on the alley-alley-o, on the last day of September.

The captain says it will never, never, do, never, never, do, never, never, do,
The captain says it will never, never, do, on the last day of September.

The big ship sank to the bottom of the sea,
        the bottom of the sea, the bottom of the sea,
The big ship sank to the bottom of the sea, on the last day of September.

Here we go Looby Loo,
Here we go Looby Light,
Here we go Looby Loo,
All on a Saturday night.
I put my right hand in,
I put my right hand out,
I give my right hand a shake, shake, shake
And turn myself about.

The north wind does blow,
And we shall have snow,
And what will poor Robin do then,
Poor thing?

He'll sit in a barn,
And keep himself warm,
And hide his head under his wing,
Poor thing.

Sing a song of sixpence,
A pocket full of rye.
Four and twenty blackbirds
Baked in a pie.

When the pie was opened,
The birds began to sing.
Wasn't that a dainty dish
To set before the King?

The King was in his counting house,
Counting out his money.
The Queen was in the parlour,
Eating bread and honey.

The maid was in the garden,
Hanging out the clothes,
When down came a blackbird
And pecked off her nose!

The Owl and the Pussycat went to sea
In a beautiful pea-green boat.
They took some honey, and plenty of money,
Wrapped up in a five-pound note.
The Owl looked up to the stars above,
And sang to a small guitar,
'O lovely Pussy! O Pussy, my love,
What a beautiful Pussy you are,
You are, you are!
What a beautiful Pussy you are!'

Three little kittens
They lost their mittens,
And they began to cry,
'Oh, mother dear,
We sadly fear
Our mittens we have lost.'
'What! Lost your mittens,
You naughty kittens!
Then you shall have no pie.'
'Mee-ow, mee-ow, mee-ow.'
'No, you shall have no pie.'

The three little kittens
They found their mittens,
And they began to cry,
'Oh, mother dear,
See here, see here,
Our mittens we have found.'
'Put on your mittens,
You silly kittens,
And you shall have some pie.'
'Purr-r, purr-r, purr-r,
Oh, let us have some pie.'

Girls and boys come out to play,
The moon is shining as bright as day.
Come with a whoop and come with a call,
Come with a good will or not at all.

Up the ladder and down the wall,
A halfpenny roll will serve us all.
You find milk and I'll find flour,
And we'll have pudding in half an hour.

Oh, dear! What can the matter be?
Dear, dear! What can the matter be?
Oh, dear! What can the matter be?
Johnny's so long at the fair.

He promised to buy me a basket of posies,
A garland of lilies, a garland of roses,
A little straw hat to set off the blue ribbons,
That tie up my bonny brown hair.

Half a pound of tuppenny rice,
Half a pound of treacle,
Mix it up and make it nice,
Pop goes the weasel!

Up and down the City Road,
In and out the Eagle,
That's the way the money goes,
Pop goes the weasel!

Every night when I go out,
The monkey's on the table;
Take a stick and knock it off,
Pop goes the weasel!

Old King Cole was a merry old soul,
And a merry old soul was he.
He called for his pipe, and he called for his bowl,
And he called for his fiddlers three.

Each fiddler he had a fiddle,
And the fiddles went tweedle-dee.
Oh, there's none so rare as can compare
With King Cole and his fiddlers three.